D0603052

from SEA TO SHINING SEA

SOUTH CAROLINA

By Dennis Brindell Fradin

CONSULTANTS

Stephen Hoffius, Director of Publications,
South Carolina Historical Society

Robert L. Hillerich, Ph.D., Consultant, Pinellas County Schools, Florida;
Visiting Professor, University of South Florida

CHILDRENS PRESS®

CHICAGO

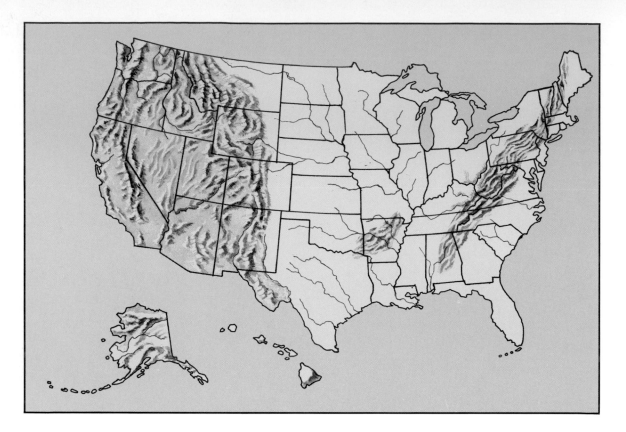

South Carolina is one of the fourteen states in the region called the South. The other southern states are Alabama, Arkansas, Delaware, Florida, Georgia, Kentucky, Louisiana, Maryland, Mississippi, North Carolina, Tennessee, Virginia, and West Virginia.

For my son, Michael Louis Fradin, with love from Dad

Front cover picture, Twickenham Plantation, Beaufort County; page 1, a deer on Hunting Island; back cover, a magnolia garden on the Ashley River

Project Editor: Joan Downing
Design Director: Karen Kohn
Research Assistant: Judith Bloom Fradin
Typesetting: Graphic Connections, Inc.
Engraving: Liberty Photoengraving

FOURTH PRINTING, 1994.

Library of Congress Cataloging-in-Publication Data

Fradin, Dennis B.
  South Carolina / by Dennis Brindell Fradin.
  p. cm. — (From sea to shining sea)
  Includes index.
  Summary: An introduction to the Palmetto State, its
geography, history, places to visit, and people.
  ISBN 0-516-03840-0
  1. South Carolina—Juvenile literature. [1. South Carolina.]
I. Title. II. Series: Fradin, Dennis B. From sea to shining sea.
F269.3.F7   1992   91-32921
917.5704'43—dc20   CIP
                                                         AC

Table of Contents

A barn in South Carolina

Introducing the Palmetto State

South Carolina is a small state in the southeastern United States. Its woods, mountains, islands, and gardens make it one of our loveliest states.

South Carolina began in the 1600s. It was one of England's thirteen American colonies. South Carolina was a rich colony. It was so rich that pirates went there to rob ships.

From 1775 to 1783, Americans fought the Revolutionary War to break free of England. In one battle, the English attacked a fort in Charleston Harbor. The fort was made of palmetto logs. It did not fall during the attack. The South Carolinians won the battle. Because of this, South Carolina is called the "Palmetto State." Nearly one hundred years later, the Civil War began in South Carolina. It was fought between the northern states and the southern states.

Today, South Carolina is a leader at making textiles (cloth goods). It is also a top state for growing tobacco and peaches.

The Palmetto State has many other claims to fame. Where were President Andrew Jackson,

The palmetto is a kind of palm tree. It is South Carolina's state tree.

children's author Peggy Parish, and civil-rights leader Jesse Jackson born? What state had the nation's first playhouse and railroad line? The answer to these questions is: South Carolina.

A picture map of South Carolina

Overleaf: Upstate mountains at dawn, Granville County

From the Mountains
to the Islands

From the Mountains to the Islands

South Carolina is one of the fourteen states that make up the region called the South. Two other southern states are its neighbors. Georgia is to the west and the south. North Carolina, its "sister state," is to the north. The Atlantic Ocean is to the east.

The Palmetto State slopes downhill from its western tip to the ocean. The state has three land regions. The smallest but highest is the Blue Ridge region. It is in the state's northwestern corner. South Carolina's only mountains are found there.

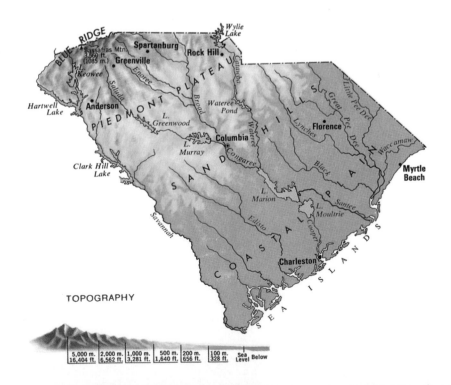

TOPOGRAPHY

| 5,000 m. | 2,000 m. | 1,000 m. | 500 m. | 200 m. | 100 m. | Sea | Below |
| 16,404 ft. | 6,562 ft. | 3,281 ft. | 1,640 ft. | 656 ft. | 328 ft. | Level | |

Among them is Sassafras Mountain. At 3,560 feet, it is the state's highest peak.

Next to the Blue Ridge is a hilly region. It is called the Piedmont. The Piedmont takes up most of the state's western half.

The state's eastern half is made up of low, rather level lands. This area is part of the Coastal Plain. Many offshore islands, including Hilton Head, Port Royal, and Kiawah, are also part of the Palmetto State.

South Carolina has many rivers. Most of them flow southeast and empty into the Atlantic Ocean. Major rivers include the Pee Dee, the Santee, the Edisto, and the Savannah.

Left: Eastatoe Gorge is in the Blue Ridge region.
Right: Sea oats grow near the ocean in the Coastal Plain.

9

Many kinds of plants and animals grow in South Carolina. Plants include spider lilies (above) and live oaks and laurel oaks (far right, middle). Among the state's animals are alligators, great blue herons, bottlenose dolphins, and buckeye butterflies.

PLANTS AND ANIMALS

Because it is in the South, the Palmetto State has a warm climate. This brings millions of vacationers to the state each year. It also gives the state many warm-weather plants and animals.

Two-thirds of South Carolina is forest. The palmetto is a tree that grows along the South Carolina coast. Cypresses, oaks, magnolias, and tulip trees grow in the swamps and lowlands. Pines, maples, hemlocks, and beeches are found inland.

Some of the cypresses and oaks look as if they are hung with grayish-green angel hair. This is Spanish moss. It is a plant that grows on trees in the South. An unusual plant that eats insects grows along the coast. It is called the Venus's-flytrap. The plant captures the insects with its leaves. Then it gives off a juice that turns the insects into food.

South Carolina's woods and waters contain many interesting animals. Dolphins often can be seen in the ocean. Alligators live in the coastal swamps. Black bears roam through the swamps and mountains. Deer and foxes live in the woods. Otters swim in the streams. Carolina wrens, pelicans, mockingbirds, catbirds, wild turkeys, geese, and ducks are among the birds that can be spotted.

North Carolina is the only other place where the Venus's-flytrap grows in the wild.

Swamps are wet, soft lands.

The Carolina wren is the state bird.

11

From Ancient Times Until Today

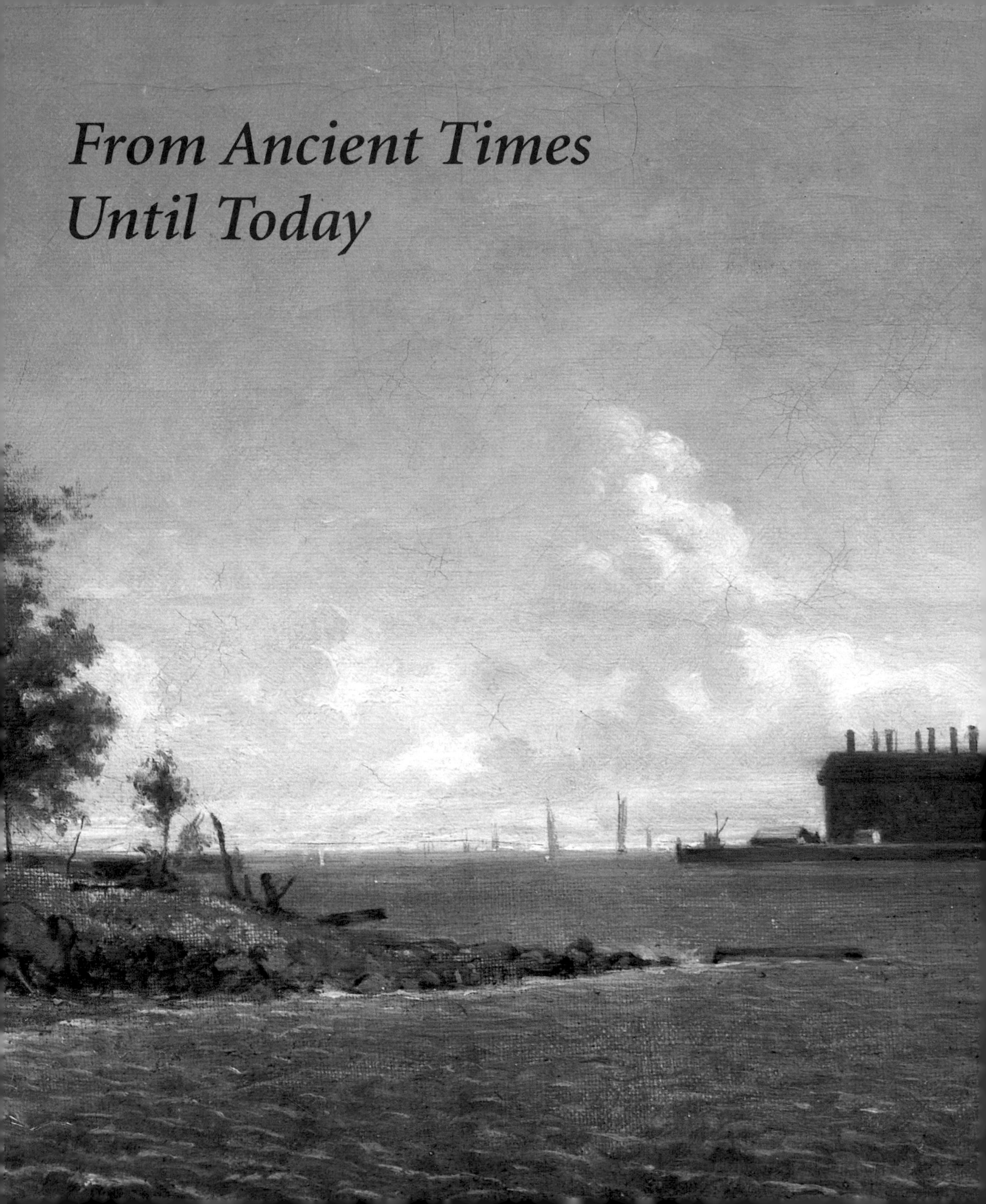

From Ancient Times Until Today

Millions of years ago, seas covered the eastern part of South Carolina. Fossils of sharks and whales have been found far from what is now the seashore. The ancient coastal beaches are now on the western edge of the Coastal Plain. They are called the Sand Hills. Columbia is in the Sand Hills region. It is in the middle of the state. In those long-ago times, it would have been on the coast.

Some animals no longer found there lived in South Carolina long ago. Fossils of camels and mammoths have been found. Mammoths were like large, hairy elephants. The last mammoths died out about the time that people first reached South Carolina.

South Carolina's American Indians

Prehistoric Indians reached South Carolina at least ten thousand years ago. At first, those early Native Americans roamed about looking for food. About three thousand years ago, they learned to farm. This enabled them to settle in villages.

Opposite: A painting of Fort Sumter, by John Ross Key

Some of the later Native American people may have been related to the ancient Indians. About fifty tribal groups lived in South Carolina before white settlers arrived. The Cherokees lived in the western mountains. The Catawbas lived in central South Carolina. Some other tribes were the Yamasees, the Westos, the Congarees, and the Kiawahs.

The Indians lived in villages. They used tree poles to build their houses. They covered the walls with bark, grass, and palmetto leaves.

The women did most of the farming. They grew corn, beans, and squash. Men hunted with bows and arrows, and fished with nets. The Indians used animals and plants for much more than food. Animal skins were turned into clothing and moccasins. Spanish moss was used to make stuffing for

Many American Indian tribes called corn, beans, and squash the "Three Sisters" because they were so important.

When artist John White visited the Carolina region in 1585, he made this drawing of an Indian village.

14

mattresses. The Indians even made a kind of aspirin from willow bark.

The Indians loved sports. The "ball game" was popular. Wooden goalposts were put in the ground. Two teams used sticks to send a deerskin ball toward each other's goal.

The "ball game" was an early form of lacrosse.

EXPLORERS AND FIRST SETTLERS

In 1492, Christopher Columbus explored for Spain. He reached some islands off Florida. Columbus thought he was near India. That is why the islands were called the West Indies. Spanish settlers soon moved to the West Indies. They began exploring the American mainland to the north.

In 1513, Juan Ponce de León reached Florida. He became the first known European in Florida. In 1521, another Spaniard, Francisco Gordillo, led the first known exploration of South Carolina. Near what is now Georgetown, Gordillo kidnapped 150 Indians. He took them to the West Indies as slaves.

One of the Indians was named Francisco Chicora. He told the Spaniards some tall tales. People with long tails lived in his homeland, Chicora said. He also said that the region was rich with gold. The Spaniards decided to settle what is now South Carolina. Lucas Vásquez de Ayllón started a colony along the coast in 1526. But disease and hunger soon brought it to an end.

France also hoped to colonize the region. A small group of French people settled near present-day Beaufort in 1562. That settlement didn't last long, either.

England was the main country to colonize America. England settled Virginia in 1607. It was the first of England's thirteen American colonies. In 1629, England's King Charles I gave a large piece of America to Sir Robert Heath. Heath named this land *Carolana* for his king. Heath tried but failed to settle Carolana. In the 1650s, some English people from Virginia moved into what is now North Carolina. But there weren't many of them. What is now South Carolina was still unsettled.

In 1663, King Charles II changed the name to *Carolina*. That year, he found a way to settle the region. He gave Carolina to eight landlords called lords proprietors. People who moved to Carolina would pay them rent.

The proprietors signed up more than a hundred people to settle South Carolina. They left England in the summer of 1669. They almost didn't get there because of storms at sea. But finally, in March

England's King Charles II

The people of Charles Town moved their belongings to a new town site in 1680.

1670, the settlers reached South Carolina. At a spot almost halfway up its coast, they began building South Carolina's first town. It was named Charles Town. Today, we spell it Charleston. Charleston was South Carolina's only permanent town for forty years.

The name Charles Town honored England's King Charles II.

COLONIAL TIMES

Charleston was not a healthful place. The land was too swampy. In 1680, the town was moved about three miles to a spot between the Ashley and Cooper rivers. Meanwhile, more people had sailed to Charleston. By 1680, about one thousand colonists lived in South Carolina.

At first, families grew corn and other crops to feed themselves. But soon they needed a crop they could sell. Rice became the colony's first "cash crop." Rice reached South Carolina by the 1680s. We're not sure how it got there. A sea captain may have brought it from Africa. Or maybe a ship carrying rice was wrecked on the South Carolina shore. However it got there, rice grew well in South Carolina's swampy coastlands. Many rice planters bought black slaves to help with their farming. Some rich families built huge farms called plantations. Dozens—sometimes even hundreds—of slaves did the work on the plantations.

Many slaves were brought to South Carolina. By about 1710, they outnumbered the white people. Life was very hard for slaves. Many of them often

For a while during the 1700s, rice was used as money in South Carolina.

All thirteen colonies allowed slavery. But there were more slaves in the South than in the North.

worked fifteen hours a day. Their homes were crowded huts. They were fed corn mush and other cheap foods. Now and then, the slaves rebelled. One huge slave revolt took place in South Carolina in 1739-1740. It was called the Stono Rebellion because it began along the Stono River. By the time it was over, about sixty slaves and thirty white people were dead.

The Indians were angry, too. The settlers kept seizing more and more of their land. In 1710, a second South Carolina town was founded. It was named Beaufort. The Indians knew the settlers would build towns everywhere unless they were stopped. Between 1715 and 1717, the Yamasees and some other tribes fought the Yamasee War against the South Carolinians. For a while, it looked as if South Carolina might be destroyed. But in the end, the colonial army defeated the Indians.

Pirates were another threat. The famous pirate Blackbeard robbed ships along the Carolina and Virginia coasts starting around 1717. He was called Blackbeard because of his long black beard, which he tied with colored ribbons. Stede Bonnet was another well-known pirate in the region. Bonnet made people "walk the plank," or jump into the ocean to die.

Charles Town was built on a peninsula between the Ashley and Cooper rivers. This painting by Andrew Melrose is called Early Morning on the Ashley River— Going to Market.

It is thought that Blackbeard's real name was Edward Teach.

Pirate Stede Bonnet was hanged in Charleston.

Blackbeard and his men robbed eight or nine ships in Charleston Harbor in mid-1718. The governors of South Carolina and Virginia then decided to end piracy. In late 1718, Blackbeard was killed in a battle along the North Carolina coast. Stede Bonnet and about fifty other pirates were captured. They were hanged in Charleston. After this, piracy was less of a threat to the Carolinas.

Some changes were made in Carolina in the early 1700s. In 1712, the colony was split into North Carolina and South Carolina. The Carolinas had not made the proprietors rich, as they had hoped. In 1719, they gave South Carolina back to the king. Ten years later, they gave up North Carolina to the king. Both Carolinas were now royal colonies. This meant that the king ruled them through his governors.

South Carolina had done well under the proprietors. It did even better as a royal colony. People moved inland and built new towns. In the 1730s, the regions that became Orangeburg and Florence were settled. In 1732, the colony's first successful newspaper began. Founded in Charleston, it was called the *South Carolina Weekly Journal.* Four years later, the Dock Street Theater opened in Charleston. It was America's first playhouse.

Eliza Lucas Pinckney helped South Carolina grow richer. Eliza lived with her parents at Wappoo Plantation, near Charleston. She liked to experiment with plants. When she was about seventeen, Eliza began growing indigo plants. A blue dye, also called indigo, came from this plant. England would pay a lot for this dye.

In the 1700s, there were no artificial dyes as we have today.

After about five years of trying. Eliza grew a good indigo crop in 1744. The news spread. Eliza shared her seeds with others. Soon, many South Carolinians were growing both rice and indigo. The two crops helped make South Carolina a very rich colony by the 1760s.

THE REVOLUTIONARY WAR ERA

In 1763, England needed money. England began taxing the Americans to raise funds. Between 1764 and 1773, the Americans were taxed on such items as paint and tea.

Americans hated these taxes. In Charleston, men formed a group called the Sons of Liberty. They fought the taxes. Christopher Gadsden belonged to the Sons of Liberty. He spoke of freeing America from England. The war to do this began in Massachusetts on April 19, 1775. About twenty-five thousand South Carolinians fought for America during this Revolutionary War. They were called patriots.

The English wanted to capture Charleston. English ships neared the town in June 1776. Thousands of South Carolinians rushed to defend Charleston. As the enemy closed in, Colonel William Moultrie and his men were building a fort to guard Charleston. Fort Moultrie was built on Sullivan's Island. The island had many palmetto trees. The patriots used the palmetto logs for the walls of the fort.

The English ships attacked Fort Moultrie on June 28, 1776. They thought the fort wouldn't last long. But the cannonballs just sank into the soft palmetto logs. Hour after hour, the two sides exchanged cannon fire. At one point, the English shot down the South Carolina flag from the fort. Sergeant William Jasper rushed from the fort. Braving enemy fire, Jasper picked up the flag and raised it above Fort Moultrie once more. The Americans won the battle at Fort Moultrie. More than two hundred enemy troops were killed or wounded. Charleston was safe—for the time being.

Six days later, on July 4, 1776, American leaders approved the Declaration of Independence. This

Sergeant William Jasper rescued the South Carolina flag after Fort Moultrie was attacked by the British in 1776. At that time, the flag was all blue except for a silver crescent with the word Liberty *in one corner.*

paper said that the thirteen colonies were now the United States. Edward Rutledge, Thomas Heyward, Jr., Thomas Lynch, Jr., and Arthur Middleton signed the Declaration for South Carolina.

Winning freedom was harder than declaring it. Major cities such as New York and Philadelphia fell to the English. In the spring of 1780, a huge English army approached Charleston by sea. Charleston and its five thousand American troops had to surrender.

The English spread out from Charleston. They took over much of South Carolina. Bands of South Carolinians fought to keep the enemy from taking the whole state.

In May 1780, the English surrounded Charleston, and the Americans were forced to surrender.

Francis Marion, the "Swamp Fox"

Francis Marion led one of these fighting bands. Marion was barely five feet tall. He limped. Yet, the English were terrified of him. Marion and his men hid in the swamps of eastern South Carolina. At times, they ran out to attack the enemy. Because of this, Marion was called the "Swamp Fox." Thomas Sumter was called the "Gamecock." He led raids in central South Carolina. Andrew Pickens raided the enemy in the western part of the state. Counties in the areas of South Carolina where they fought were named for Marion, Sumter, and Pickens.

Meanwhile, American forces tried to win back South Carolina. Three big battles were fought in the state near the end of the war. The Battle of Camden (August 16, 1780) was an awful American loss. But the Americans won great victories at the battles of Kings Mountain (October 7, 1780) and Cowpens (January 17, 1781). At Kings Mountain, the Americans killed, wounded, or captured all eleven hundred English troops. General Daniel Morgan and his men did much the same to the enemy at Cowpens.

The two big victories in South Carolina helped America win the war. The English forces withdrew to Yorktown, Virginia. There, in October 1781, George Washington's army beat them in the war's last big battle. The peace treaty was signed in 1783. The United States had won its freedom.

THE EIGHTH STATE

In 1787, American leaders drew up the United States Constitution. It established basic laws for the country. South Carolinians John Rutledge, Pierce Butler, and cousins Charles Pinckney and Charles Cotesworth Pinckney helped create this framework of government. Each state would officially join the country when it approved the Constitution. South Carolina became the eighth state on May 23, 1788.

The first South Carolina State House, in Columbia, was finished in late 1790.

By the late 1700s, about as many settlers lived in the state's western half as in its eastern half. Lawmakers in the west found it hard to reach Charleston, on the coast. Charleston had been the capital since 1670. In 1790, the capital was moved to Columbia. That was a new town in the middle of the state.

SLAVERY AND CIVIL WAR

In 1793, Eli Whitney invented the cotton gin. This machine could clean cotton fifty times as fast as a person cleaning it by hand. It made cotton grow-

Slaves bringing in the cotton from the fields

ing very profitable. Cotton became so important to the South that it was called "King Cotton." By 1820, Georgia and South Carolina together were growing more than half the nation's cotton.

There was a tragic result. More workers were needed on the cotton plantations. White planters decided to use more slave labor. By 1850, nearly 400,000 of South Carolina's 670,000 people were slaves. The northern states had ended slavery by then. Most northerners wanted the South to end it, too. But white southerners felt that each state had the right to decide issues like slavery for itself. South Carolina's John C. Calhoun was the leading speaker for "states' rights."

Finally, eleven southern states seceded from (left) the country. South Carolina seceded first, on December 20, 1860. The eleven southern states formed the Confederate States of America, or the Confederacy. On the morning of April 12, 1861, the Confederates fired on Fort Sumter. That was a United States fort in Charleston Harbor. This began America's deadliest war to this day. The Civil War (1861-1865) was fought between the Confederacy (the South) and the Union (the North).

More than sixty thousand South Carolinians fought for the Confederacy. One clash took place in

Charleston Harbor on February 17, 1864. That day, the Confederate submarine *Hunley* sank the Union ship *Housatonic*. This was the first sinking of a warship by a submarine.

The Confederates weren't strong enough to win the war, though. South Carolina suffered as the end neared for the South. In early 1865, Union forces seized Charleston. They burned Columbia. They wrecked many South Carolina farms. By the time the war ended on April 9, 1865, about fifteen thousand of South Carolina's troops had died. The one good result of the war was the freeing of the slaves.

After the war, the United States began what it called Reconstruction of the South. Blacks gained

Left: The Civil War began on April 12, 1861, when Confederates fired on Fort Sumter, in Charleston Harbor. Right: Fort Sumter today

the right to vote. They elected many blacks to the South Carolina legislature. Northerners came down to make sure that South Carolina obeyed United States laws. Some were dishonest men who hurt rather than helped the state. Finally, in June 1868, South Carolina rejoined the United States. South Carolinians then rebuilt their own state. However, whites in the state took from blacks the right to vote. A system of segregation—separation of the races—was established.

Building Modern South Carolina

South Carolinians faced many big problems. By the late 1800s, indigo and rice were no longer important to South Carolina. And without slave labor, cotton was no longer king. Thousands of South Carolinians—both blacks and whites—grew cotton on small farms. Many of these people were very poor. Beetles called boll weevils made things worse in the 1920s. They ruined much of the cotton crop.

The cloud had a silver lining. South Carolinians began growing other crops besides cotton. By 1930, farmers were growing tobacco, wheat, corn, peanuts, peaches, watermelons, and potatoes.

South Carolinians also turned to manufacturing. There had been little industry in South Carolina during its first century of statehood. This began to change around 1880. Dozens of textile mills were built in the state. They made cotton into cloth. Furniture factories were also built. By 1925, South Carolina led the nation in making cotton textiles. During World War I (1914-1918) and World War II (1939-1945), the Palmetto State produced large amounts of cloth for the American troops.

Manufacturing has kept growing since the end of World War II. Large numbers of South Carolinians have moved from farms to cities to work in the factories. In 1980, for the first time, more South Carolinians lived in cities than in farm areas.

The 1903 picture on the left shows the spinning room of a textile mill that turned cotton (below) into cloth.

In 1948, these residents of Columbia stood in line to vote in the Democratic primary election. It was the first time blacks had been allowed to vote in South Carolina elections since 1876.

But well into the 1900s, the state still had a big problem. White southerners denied black people their rights. Black adults were kept from voting. Black children had to attend separate schools. Most of those schools were not as good as the schools attended by white children. As late as the mid-1900s, there were even two Palmetto State Fairs. One was for white people. The other was for black people.

Starting in the 1950s, the United States made laws to end racial injustice. Black southerners again began to vote. In 1970, three black people were elected to South Carolina's legislature. John Felder, Herbert Fielding, and I. S. Levy Johnson were the first black people in seventy years to be legislators in the state. By 1970, many of South Carolina's schools were integrated. This meant that black children and white children attended the same schools.

South Carolina's schools still had problems. In 1980, South Carolina's students ranked low in reading, writing, and arithmetic. In 1984, South Carolina passed the Education Improvement Act. This new law created many programs to help students. It has already improved the state's schools. South Carolina hopes to have a very good school system within ten years.

Other recent South Carolina news hasn't been as pleasant. In 1953, the Savannah River Plant began operating near Aiken. It makes materials for nuclear bombs. In the 1980s, it was learned that nuclear materials had leaked from the plant. Work is being done to clean up the plant and make it safer. This work will last well past the year 2000.

Sea storms called hurricanes sometimes strike South Carolina. In September 1989, Hurricane Hugo slammed into the state. Its 135-mile-per-hour winds sent huge waves crashing into the coast. About twenty South Carolinians were killed by the water and the wind. About forty thousand homes were damaged or destroyed. The rebuilding project may take until well into the 1990s.

The wind and water of Hurricane Hugo killed about twenty people in South Carolina and caused a great amount of damage. If not for the nation's hurricane warning system, many more people would have been killed.

31

South Carolinians and Their Work

SOUTH CAROLINIANS AND THEIR WORK

South Carolina had about 3.5 million people as of 1990. It ranks twenty-fifth among the states in population. More than a million South Carolinians are black. White South Carolinians are of English, Scottish, Irish, German, French, Italian, Polish, and many other backgrounds. The state also has about ten thousand Native Americans.

Manufacturing is important in South Carolina. The only states that make more textiles are North Carolina and Georgia. Other leading products include chemicals, computers and other machinery, paper goods, and packaged foods.

Nearly as many South Carolinians sell products in stores as make them. Government work is also important. One reason for this is that the state has several military bases. Millions of tourists visit South Carolina each year. They provide thousands of hotel and restaurant jobs.

About twenty-five thousand Palmetto State families live on farms. South Carolina is one of the five leading tobacco-growing states. South Carolina's other leading crops include peaches, soybeans, corn, and cotton.

Only Mississippi has a larger percentage of African Americans than South Carolina.

South Carolina is one of the five leading tobacco-growing states.

33

A Trip Through
South Carolina

A TRIP THROUGH SOUTH CAROLINA

Pages 34-35: The Blacksmith Shop at the History Farm in Kings Mountain State Park

Charles Towne Landing is the site of the first permanent English settlement in South Carolina. One of the exhibits there is this replica of a colonial trading ship.

The Palmetto State is a wonderful place to visit. It has beautiful beaches and mountains. It has interesting cities. The state is known for its lovely plantations and gardens. South Carolina also has many famous historic sites.

SEACOAST AND ISLANDS

Charleston would be a good place to begin a trip through the Palmetto State. Charleston is South Carolina's second-largest city, after Columbia. It is also the state's oldest town. Charles Towne Landing is a historical park on the site of the 1670 settlement. A zoo in the park has wolves, alligators, and other animals that lived in South Carolina in 1670.

Boat tours take people to the famous landmarks in Charleston Harbor. Fort Sumter, where the Civil War began, is there. The original palmetto-log Fort Moultrie on Sullivan's Island is gone. However, a reconstruction of that fort is open to visitors.

George Washington visited Charleston in 1791. Many buildings the first president saw are still standing. Washington stayed at the home of

Thomas Heyward, Jr. Heyward signed the Declaration of Independence. The home is now called the Heyward-Washington House. The president worshipped at St. Michael's Episcopal Church, which dates from 1752. He watched a parade in his honor from the steps of the Old Exchange Building.

Charleston has some important "firsts" to its credit. The Dock Street Theater, which opened in 1736, was America's first playhouse. It burned in 1740, but a new Dock Street Theater stands on the site. The Charleston Museum, founded in 1773, is the nation's oldest museum. In 1831, the nation's first railroad line opened in Charleston.

Among the Charleston area's finest plantations are Middleton Place (left) and Boone Hall (right).

Below: Brick slave cabins at Boone Hall

Some lovely old plantations can be visited in the Charleston area. Boone Hall was once a cotton plantation. Cabins where slaves lived can be seen on its grounds. The Charleston area is also famous for its gardens. Among the prettiest are Cypress Gardens, Magnolia Gardens, and Middleton Place Gardens.

Georgetown is 60 miles up the coast from Charleston. Georgetown's Rice Museum is a good place to learn about the little grains that helped make South Carolina rich. Hopsewee Plantation is near Georgetown. It was the birthplace of Thomas Lynch, Jr. He was a signer of the Declaration of Independence.

Beaufort is the state's second-oldest town. It is 50 miles down the coast from Charleston. The John Mark Verdier House is in Beaufort. It was built about 1790. Union forces used it as their headquarters during the Civil War. Penn School Historic District and Museum is near Beaufort on St. Helena Island. Penn School was founded in 1862. It was the South's first school for freed slaves.

Long ago, the many islands off the South Carolina mainland were cut off from the world. Some black islanders developed their own customs. These people are sometimes called the Gullahs. Their language, also called Gullah, blends African and English words. The Gullahs are expert basket weavers. They are also known for their songs and stories.

A South Carolina basket weaver

Today, the coastal islands can be reached by bridges and boats. There are many vacation resorts on the islands and along the coast. Myrtle Beach, Hilton Head Island, and Edisto Island are popular resort areas.

THE REST OF THE ATLANTIC COASTAL PLAIN

West of Charleston there are no major cities until Columbia. There are small towns and cities, though. Many of them have an interesting history. For example, Sumter was named for Thomas Sumter (the "Gamecock"), who lived in the area. Florence had a Civil War battle. Darlington is known for a more modern event. The Southern 500 stock-car race is held there every Labor Day weekend.

The eastern half of the state is also a farming region. Tobacco farms can be seen in many places. Soybeans, corn, and cotton are some of the other crops that are grown in the area.

South Carolina's largest city is Columbia. It is located in almost the exact center of the state. Founded in 1786, Columbia became the state capital in 1790. The name *Columbia* is a nickname for the United States. It comes from the name of the famous explorer Christopher Columbus.

Hilton Head Island (above) and Myrtle Beach (below) are popular vacation areas.

Chemicals, packaged foods, computers, and textiles are made in Columbia.

The South Carolina State House is in Columbia. That is where laws are made for the Palmetto State. There are six bronze stars on the State House walls. They mark spots where Union cannonballs hit the building during the Civil War.

South Carolina's biggest museum is in Columbia. It is the South Carolina State Museum. The museum has displays on the state's animals, plants, and history. The Woodrow Wilson Boyhood Home is another highlight of Columbia. Wilson lived in Columbia as a teenager. He later became the twenty-eighth president of the United States.

In 1990, Columbia celebrated its two-hundredth anniversary as South Carolina's capital. The present State House (above) was begun in the 1850s.

The South Carolina State Museum has a life-size model of a 43-foot-long prehistoric shark that lived in South Carolina's waters.

41

The Piedmont

The Piedmont is South Carolina's main manufacturing area. It is also a farming area. Peaches, corn, and other fruits and vegetables are grown there. The Piedmont is also an important region for mining the very hard rock called granite.

Rock Hill is in the far northern part of the state. It was founded in 1852 as a railroad station. The town was named for a small rocky hill. Today, Rock Hill has more than forty thousand people. It is the state's seventh-biggest city.

A lovely plantation home called the White House is in Rock Hill. The White House was built by the White family in the 1830s. It is one of Rock Hill's oldest houses.

Kings Mountain National Military Park is near Rock Hill. During the Revolutionary War, British troops were stationed on Kings Mountain. "God Almighty could not drive us from the mountain!" their leader bragged. But in the fall of 1780, the Americans won a great victory at the Battle of Kings Mountain.

Andrew Jackson State Park is also near Rock Hill. The seventh president of the United States was born near the park. Exactly where is not known. An

South Carolina's Piedmont is an important peach-growing area.

Andrew Jackson museum and a statue of "Old Hickory" are in the park.

Spartanburg is 50 miles west of Rock Hill. Settled in 1761, it was named for the Spartan Regiment. That unit fought in the Revolutionary War. Spartanburg is the state's fifth-biggest city. It is a textile-making center.

Walnut Grove Plantation is outside Spartanburg. Revolutionary War heroine Kate Barry lived there as a child. During the war, Barry rode through the countryside rounding up patriots to fight the British. She recruited men for the Battle of Cowpens. This battle was fought near Spartanburg in early 1781.

Andrew Jackson was called "Old Hickory" because people said that he was as tough and strong as hickory wood.

Below: A pavilion at Andrew Jackson State Park

Spools of thread like these are used to make cloth in textile centers such as Greenville.

Rafting on the Chattooga River, in the Blue Ridge

Greenville, the state's fourth-biggest city, is southwest of Spartanburg. It was named for Revolutionary War hero Nathanael Greene. Greenville is called the "Textile Center of the World." Clothing, thread, and bedspreads are among the many textile goods made there. Greenville was also the birthplace of civil-rights leader Jesse Jackson.

THE BLUE RIDGE MOUNTAINS

One look and people know how the Blue Ridge Mountains got their name. They really do look blue from a distance. The color comes from trees on the mountainsides. The Blue Ridge is a popular place to camp, hike, raft, and fish.

Caesars Head is a famous Blue Ridge mountain. It looks somewhat like a head. Some people think that the mountain was named for Julius Caesar, the Roman emperor. Others say that it was named for a dog called Caesar.

Sassafras Mountain, the state's highest peak, is near Caesars Head. Also nearby is Table Rock Mountain. The Cherokee Indians say that a giant chief used this mountain as a table. Another mountain called "The Stool" was said to be his chair.

In places, waterfalls tumble down through the highlands. Whitewater Falls is lovely. It is actually two waterfalls. One is on the North Carolina side of the border. The other is on the South Carolina side. Both are more than 400 feet high. They are among the highest waterfalls in the eastern United States.

The city of Clemson is in the far western part of the state. It is home to Clemson University. Fort Hill is on the university's grounds. It was the home of John C. Calhoun, once a vice-president of the United States.

Above: The team flag of the Clemson University Tigers is displayed at a football game.

The city of Clemson and the university were both named for Thomas Clemson, who left money that helped found the university.

A Gallery
of Famous
South
Carolinians

A GALLERY OF FAMOUS SOUTH CAROLINIANS

South Carolina has been home to many famous people. They range from politicians to plant experts. **Henry Woodward** (1646?-1686?) may have been born on the English-ruled island of Barbados. He became a surgeon at a young age. Dr. Woodward moved to North Carolina when he was about twenty. In mid-1666, he left to explore South Carolina. Friendly Indians along the coast asked Dr. Woodward to live with them for a time. He agreed, thus becoming South Carolina's first permanent European settler. Woodward helped found Charleston a few years later.

In the 1600s, it took little training to become a surgeon.

Eliza Lucas Pinckney (1722-1793) was probably born on the English-ruled island of Antigua. When Eliza was about fifteen, she and her family settled near Charleston. Eliza's father had to return to Antigua. Her mother was ill, so sixteen-year-old Eliza had to run the family's three plantations. While doing so, Eliza began the indigo industry. Her sons, Charles Cotesworth Pinckney and Thomas Pinckney, became famous statesmen.

Alexander Garden (1730-1791) was born in Scotland. He became a naturalist and moved to

Opposite: A painting of Andrew Jackson on his horse, Sam Patch

South Carolina. Garden collected plants and animals. He discovered some animals in South Carolina, including the mud iguana. To honor Garden for his work, the flower called the gardenia was named for him.

Christopher Gadsden (1724-1805) was born in Charleston. He became a rich merchant and a lawmaker. Gadsden was one of the first Americans to favor independence. He helped found the U.S. Navy during the Revolutionary War. The British captured Gadsden in 1780. The "Flame of Liberty," as he was called, spent about a year in a dungeon. After his release, Gadsden was elected governor of South Carolina. But prison had ruined his health and he couldn't serve.

Andrew Jackson (1767-1845) was born in the Waxhaw community, thought to have been in South Carolina. (Some North Carolinians think he was born in their state.) At the age of thirteen, Jackson joined a South Carolina unit that was fighting the British. He was captured. A British officer ordered Jackson to clean his boots. When Jackson refused, the officer cut him with his sword. Later, Andrew Jackson became an officer and a lawmaker. From 1829 to 1837, "Old Hickory" served as the seventh president of the United States.

Christopher Gadsden

Robert Mills (1781-1855) was born in Charleston. In 1800, he moved to Washington, D.C., which became the capital of the United States that very year. Mills became a great architect and studied with Thomas Jefferson. He designed the Washington Monument in Washington, D.C., that honors our first president.

Robert Mills

John C. Calhoun (1782-1850) was born in what is now Abbeville County. He had little schooling until he went to a log school at the age of eighteen. Calhoun was elected to the state legislature when he was only twenty-six years old. He later served as U.S. secretary of war, secretary of state, and vice-president.

John C. Calhoun

Mary McLeod Bethune (left) founded Bethune-Cookman College. Today, the college has many other programs besides teacher-training classes.

Mary McLeod Bethune (1875-1955) was born in Mayesville. Her parents had been slaves. She became a teacher. In 1904, she founded what became Bethune-Cookman College in Florida, a leading school for training black teachers. From 1936 to 1944, Bethune headed a U.S. agency that helped young black people obtain education and work. She was the first black woman to head a U. S. government agency.

Strom Thurmond was born in Edgefield in 1902. He taught high school for six years before becoming a politician. As South Carolina's governor from 1947 to 1951, Thurmond improved the state's schools. In 1954, he was elected to the U. S.

Senate. In 1991, Strom Thurmond was the Senate's oldest member. He was eighty-nine.

Jesse Jackson was born in Greenville in 1941. He became a preacher and a civil-rights leader. In 1971, he founded PUSH. That is a group that works for the rights of black people. Jackson has continued to work for this cause in many ways.

South Carolina is shaped a little like a baseball diamond, with Columbia as the pitcher's mound. So it makes sense that some great baseball players have come from there. **Larry Doby** was born in Camden

Jesse Jackson

Senator Strom Thurmond shaking hands with supporters in 1954

"Shoeless Joe" Jackson (left) got his nickname when he played without shoes because of a sore foot. Althea Gibson (right) was a star tennis player in the 1950s.

in 1923. He joined the Cleveland Indians in 1947. He was the American League's first black player. Doby led the league in homers in 1952 and 1954. Then in 1978, he became the American League's first black manager. **"Shoeless Joe" Jackson** (1888-1951) and **Jim Rice** (born in 1953) were two other baseball greats from the Palmetto State.

Althea Gibson was born in Silver in 1927. She was one of the best women tennis players of the 1950s. Later, she became a pro golfer. Race-car driver **Cale Yarborough** was born in Timmonsville in 1939. Heavyweight boxing champ **Joe Frazier** was born in Beaufort in 1944.

Eartha Kitt is one of the best entertainers to come from the Palmetto State. She was born in North in about 1928. Eartha Kitt became a famous singer, dancer, and actress.

One South Carolina woman has made millions of young readers happy. Her name was **Peggy Parish** (1927-1988), and she was born in Manning. Parish taught third grade for many years. Later, she wrote children's books. Parish is best known for her Amelia Bedelia books about a very funny maid.

Home to Andrew Jackson, Jesse Jackson, Eliza Pinckney, Alexander Garden, and Peggy Parish . . .

Site of the nation's first playhouse and railroad line . . .

The place where the "Swamp Fox" helped beat the British and where the Civil War began . . .

A state once famous for rice and cotton, but now known for textiles and tobacco . . .

This is South Carolina—the Palmetto State!

Race-car driver Cale Yarborough

Heavyweight boxing champ Joe Frazier

Did You Know?

The Christmas plants called poinsettias were named for Joel Poinsett, who was born in Charleston. Poinsett first brought the plant to the United States from Mexico.

The beautiful green, orange, and yellow Carolina parakeet was named for the Carolinas. Hunted for their feathers, the last of these birds was killed in the early 1900s.

The dance called the Charleston was named for Charleston, South Carolina.

Mary McLeod Bethune was the fifteenth of seventeen children.

South Carolina has towns named Four Holes, Ninety Six, Round O, Seven Oaks, and Six Mile.

Other South Carolina towns include Blacksburg, Blue Brick, Gray Court, Greenwood, Orangeburg, Red Bank, and White Rock.

Every summer, more than one hundred hot-air balloons are launched over Greenville during a balloonists' festival called Freedom Weekend Aloft.

In 1984, the shag was chosen as South Carolina's official dance. Performed to rhythm-and-blues music, it was developed along the South Carolina coast in the 1940s.

Captain Chicken was a leading soldier of colonial South Carolina. His first name was George.

Eliza Lucas Pinckney taught her son Charles to spell before he was two years old.

The Best Friend of Charleston was a locomotive on the nation's first railroad line. It went about 20 miles per hour. In 1990, Dale Earnhardt won the Southern 500 stock-car race in Darlington with an average speed of 123 miles per hour.

South Carolina's Jim Rice led the American League in homers three times. He belted thirty-nine in 1977, forty-six in 1978, and thirty-nine in 1983.

Among other things, South Carolina's Eartha Kitt played the Cat Woman on the "Batman" television show.

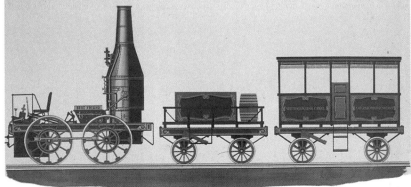

SOUTH CAROLINA INFORMATION

The state flag

Area: 31,113 square miles (fortieth among the states in size)

Greatest Distance North to South: 218 miles

Greatest Distance East to West: 275 miles

Coastline: 187 miles

Borders: North Carolina to the north; the Atlantic Ocean to the east; Georgia to the south and west

Highest Point: Sassafras Mountain, 3,560 feet above sea level

Lowest Point: Sea level, along the shore of the Atlantic Ocean

Hottest Recorded Temperature: 111° F. (at Blackville on September 4, 1925; Calhoun Falls on September 8, 1925; and Camden on June 28, 1954)

Coldest Recorded Temperature: -20° F. (at Caesars Head on January 18, 1977)

Statehood: The eighth state, on May 23, 1788

Origin of Name: North and South Carolina were named in honor of England's King Charles I; the name comes from *Carolana* (Latin, meaning "Land of Charles")

Capital: Columbia (since 1790)

Previous Capital: Charleston (1670-1790)

Counties: 46

United States Representatives: 6 (as of 1992)

State Senators: 46

State Representatives: 124

State Songs: "Carolina," by Henry Timrod (words) and Anne Custis Burgess (music); and "South Carolina on My Mind," by Hank Martin and Buzz Arledge

State Mottoes: *Animis Opibusque Parati* (Latin, meaning "Prepared in mind and resources"); and *Dum Spiro Spero* (Latin, meaning "While I breathe, I hope"

Palmetto trees

Nickname: Palmetto State

State Seal: Adopted in 1776

State Flag: Adopted in 1861

State Flower: Carolina yellow jessamine

State Bird: Carolina wren

State Tree: Palmetto

State Animal: White-tailed deer

State Reptile: Loggerhead sea turtle

State Insect: Carolina mantid

State Fish: Striped bass

State Stone: Blue granite

State Wild Game Bird: Wild turkey

State Fruit: Peach

State Beverage: Milk

State Dance: The shag

State Dog: Boykin spaniel

Some Rivers: Pee Dee, Santee, Cooper, Wando, Edisto, Wateree, Congaree, Savannah, Broad, Saluda

Some Islands: Daufuskie, Hilton Head, Port Royal, St. Helena, Edisto, Kiawah, Isle of Palms

Wildlife: Black bears, deer, foxes, opossums, raccoons, minks, otters, skunks, alligators, loggerhead sea turtles and other turtles, wild turkeys, Carolina wrens, mockingbirds, catbirds, pelicans, herons, egrets, hundreds of other kinds of birds, rattlesnakes, water moccasins, other snakes, whales, dolphins, bass, trout, many other kinds of fish

Fishing Products: Shrimp, oysters, crabs, clams

Farm Products: Tobacco, peaches, soybeans, corn, cotton, wheat, tomatoes, beef cattle, dairy cattle, hogs, chickens, eggs, turkeys

Mining: Granite, limestone, clay

Manufactured Products: Many kinds of textiles, chemicals, computers, machinery, paper goods, car tires, packaged foods

Population: 3,486,703, twenty-fifth among the states (1990 U.S. Census Bureau figures)

Major Cities (1990 Census):

Columbia	98, 052	Spartanburg	43, 467
Charleston	80, 414	Sumter	41, 943
North Charleston	70, 218	Rock Hill	41, 643
Greenville	58, 282		

Carolina yellow jessamine

White-tailed deer

SOUTH CAROLINA HISTORY

About 10,000 B.C.—Prehistoric Indians live in South Carolina

1521—Spaniard Francisco Gordillo leads the first known exploration of the South Carolina coast

1526—Spaniards build the first known European settlement in South Carolina

1562—The French found an outpost near present-day Beaufort

1629—England's King Charles I grants Carolana to Sir Robert Heath, who fails to settle the region

1663—The spelling of Carolana is changed to *Carolina*; England's King Charles II gives Carolina to eight lords proprietors (landlords)

1670—Charleston is founded

1712—North and South Carolina are made separate colonies

1719—South Carolina becomes a royal colony

1744—Eliza Lucas Pinckney begins the indigo industry in South Carolina

1775—The Revolutionary War begins

1776—The English try but fail to capture Fort Moultrie

1780—The English take Charleston; the English win the Battle of Camden; the Americans win the Battle of Kings Mountain

1781—The Americans win the Battle of Cowpens

1783—The Americans win the Revolutionary War

1788—South Carolina becomes the eighth state on May 23

1790—Columbia becomes the state capital

1805—The University of South Carolina opens in Columbia

1825—John C. Calhoun becomes vice-president of the United States

1828—Andrew Jackson is elected the seventh president of the United States

1850—The population of the Palmetto State reaches 670,000

The University of South Carolina opened in 1805.

58

1860—South Carolina becomes the first state to secede from the Union

1861—The Civil War begins at Fort Sumter in Charleston Harbor

1865—Union forces seize Charleston and burn Columbia; the Confederacy loses the war

1868—South Carolina rejoins the United States

1893—A hurricane kills between one thousand and two thousand people along the South Carolina coast

1895—South Carolina adopts its present state constitution

1900—The population of the Palmetto State reaches 1.3 million

1917-18—About sixty-five thousand South Carolinians serve during World War I

1924—A tornado kills about seventy South Carolinians

1941-45—About two hundred thousand South Carolinians help the United States and its allies win World War II

1955—Tobacco replaces cotton as South Carolina's leading crop

1963—A black student enters Clemson University; the public schools are also being integrated

1964—The Civil Rights Act of 1964 helps blacks find work in the textile industry

1970—Charleston celebrates its 300th birthday; the first black people in seventy years are elected to the South Carolina House of Representatives

1983—The Reverend I. DeQuincy Newman is the first black person elected to the South Carolina Senate in about one hundred years

1984—Tornadoes kill about sixty people in the Carolinas; South Carolina passes the Education Improvement Act

1988—South Carolina celebrates its 200th birthday as a state

1989—Hurricane Hugo kills about twenty South Carolinians and damages or destroys about forty thousand homes

1990—The population of the Palmetto State reaches 3.5 million

Confederate militiamen posing with captured guns at Fort Sumter

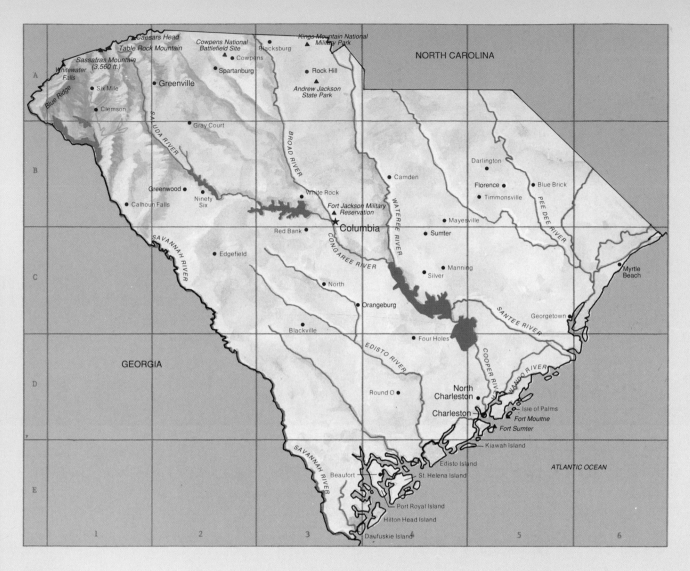

MAP KEY

GLOSSARY

ancient: Relating to those living at a time early in history

architect: A building planner

capital: The city that is the seat of government

cash crop: A crop that can be sold

civil rights: The rights of a citizen

climate: The weather of a region

coast: The land along a large body of water

colonize: To found a colony

colony: A settlement outside a parent country and ruled by the parent country

Confederacy: A short name for the Confederate States of America, the country the South formed at the start of the Civil War

Declaration of Independence: The paper stating that the United States was free of England

explorers: People who visit and study unknown lands

fossils: Remains of animals or plants that lived long ago

frontier: A place that has just started to become developed

gamecock: A fighting rooster

granite: A kind of rock known for its hardness

heroine: A woman admired for her bravery or great deeds

hurricanes: Huge storms that form over oceans

independence: Freedom from the control or support of others

inland: Away from the shore; toward the interior

integrate: To make schools, parks, and other such places available to people of all races

legislature: Lawmaking body

locomotive: The part of a train that pulls the other cars

manufacturing: The making of products

milestone: An important event

million: A thousand thousand (1,000,000)

moccasins: Soft shoes made of animal skins

patriots: People who love and support their country

permanent: Lasting

pirates: Robbers who operate on the high seas

population: The number of people in a place

prehistoric: Before written history

profitable: Money-making

settlers: People who move to an uninhabited area

slaves: People who are owned by other people

tourists: People who visit a place

tragic: Very sad or terrible

United States Constitution: The framework of government for the United States

PICTURE ACKNOWLEDGMENTS

Front cover, © Janice S. Sauls/**Stock Portfolio, Inc.;** 1, © Robert C. Clark/**Stock Portfolio, Inc.;** 2, **Tom Dunnington;** 3, © Robert C. Clark/**Stock Portfolio, Inc.;** 4-5, **Tom Dunnington;** 6-7, © Bill Tuttle/**Stock Portfolio, Inc.;** 8, **Courtesy Hammond Incorporated, Maplewood, New Jersey;** 9 (both pictures), © Robert C. Clark/**Stock Portfolio, Inc.;** 10 (top left, middle, middle right, bottom right), © Robert C. Clark/**Stock Portfolio, Inc.;** 10 (top right, bottom left), © Brian Parker/**Tom Stack & Associates;** 11, © Skip Moody/**Dembinsky Photo Associates;** 12, **Robert M. Hicklin, Jr., Inc., Spartanburg, South Carolina,** 14, **North Wind Picture Archives;** 16, **North Wind Picture Archives;** 17, **North Wind Picture Archives;** 18, **North Wind Picture Archives;** 19, **Robert M. Hicklin, Jr., Inc., Spartanburg, South Carolina;** 20, from the collections of the **South Carolina Historical Society;** 22, **North Wind Picture Archives;** 23, from the collections of the **South Carolina Historical Society;** 24, **North Wind Picture Archives;** 25, from the collections of the **South Carolina Historical Society;** 26, from the collections of the **South Carolina Historical Society;** 27 (left), from the collections of the **South Carolina Historical Society;** 27 (right), © **SuperStock;** 29 (left), **South Carolina State Museum;** 29 (right), **AP/Wide World Photos;** 30, **AP/Wide World Photos;** 31, © Joseph Jacobson/**Journalism Services;** 32, © **Joan Dunlop;** 33 (top), © **Jeff Greenberg;** 33 (bottom), © **Eric Futran Photography;** 34-35, © Bill Tuttle/**Stock Portfolio, Inc.;** 36, © **Photri;** 37 (left), © **Photri;** 37 (right) © Robert C. Clark/**Stock Portfolio, Inc.;** 38 (top left), © Robert C. Clark/**Stock Portfolio, Inc.;** 38 (top right), © R. Krubner/© **H. Armstrong Roberts;** 38 (bottom), © D & I MacDonald/**Photri;** 39, © Jon Riley/**Tony Stone Worldwide/Chicago Ltd.;** 40 (top), © R. Kord/**H. Armstrong Roberts;** 40 (bottom), © Robert C. Clark/**Stock Portfolio, Inc.;** 41, © **Gene Ahrens;** 42, © Robert C. Clark/**Stock Portfolio, Inc.;** 43, © Bill Tuttle/**Stock Portfolio, Inc.;** 44 (top), © Robert C. Clark/**Stock Portfolio, Inc.;** 44 (bottom), © Michael Foster/**Stock Portfolio, Inc.;** 45, © Bill Howe/**Photri;** 46, **The Hermitage: Home of President Andrew Jackson, Nashville, Tennessee;** 48, **Painting by Rembrandt Peale, Courtesy Independence National Historical Park;** 49 (top), **Dictionary of American Portraits;** 49 (bottom), **Historical Pictures Service, Chicago;** 50, **Historical Pictures Service, Chicago;** 51 (top), **AP/Wide World Photos;** 51 (bottom), **UPI/Bettmann Newsphotos;** 52 (both pictures), **AP/Wide World Photos;** 53 (both pictures), **AP/Wide World Photos;** 54 (bottom left), **courtesy of Douglas Kenyon, Inc., Chicago;** 54-55 (top), **UPI-Bettmann;** 55 (top right), **Wide World Photos, Inc.;** 55 (bottom right), **Norfolk Southern Corporation;** 56 (top), **courtesy Flag Research Center, Winchester, Massachusetts, 01890;** 56 (bottom), © Robert C. Clark/**Stock Portfolio, Inc.;** 57 (top), © Bill Tuttle/**Stock Portfolio, Inc.;** 57 (bottom), © Thomas Kitchin/**Tom Stack & Associates;** 58, **University of South Carolina, University Publications;** 59, **manuscripts section, Howard-Tilton Memorial Library, Tulane University/Louisiana Historical Association Collection;** 60, **Tom Dunnington;** back cover, © **Tom Till**

INDEX

Page numbers in boldface type indicate illustrations.

ABOUT THE AUTHOR

Dennis Brindell Fradin is the author of more than one hundred published children's books. His works for Childrens Press include the Young People's Stories of Our States series, the Disaster! series, and the Thirteen Colonies series. His other books are *Remarkable Children* (Little, Brown) and *How I Saved the World* (Dillon). Dennis is married to Judith Bloom Fradin, a high-school English teacher. They have two sons, Tony and Mike, and a daughter, Diana. Dennis graduated from Northwestern University in 1967 with a B.A. in creative writing, and has lived in Evanston, Illinois, since that year.